EUROPA ⚔ MILITARIA Nº 22

D1757440

IFOR: ALLIED FORCES IN BOSNIA

CARL SCHULZE

Windrow & Greene

© Carl Schulze 1996

Designed by John Anastasio/Creative Line
Printed in Spain

This edition published
in Great Britain 1996 by
Windrow & Greene Ltd.
5 Gerrard Street
London W1V 7LJ

All rights reserved. No part of this publication
may be reproduced or transmitted in any form or
by any means electronic or mechanical, including
photocopy, recording, or in any information
storage and retrieval system, without the prior
written permission of the publishers.

A CIP catalogue record for this book
is available from the British Library

ISBN 1 85915 008 X

Author's note:
The information in this book relates to the structure and major combat units of IFOR during its deployment to Bosnia-Herzegovina in January-March 1996. Available space does not allow examination of the whole of this huge and complex military organisation; and the picture is further complicated by the rotation principle followed by most contributing nations - individual units stay in theatre no longer than five months before replacement by other units of the same, or sometimes even a different nation. This book can therefore only be a "snapshot"; all the pictures were taken between 16 February and 7 March 1996, just before one of the major deadlines of the Peace Agreement for the handing back of occupied areas to the former populations. As the operation continues deployment of units to new operational areas is quite common; and certain information, e.g. regarding exact strengths, has to be omitted, since the safety and success of the soldiers serving with IFOR must naturally take priority. I can only ask for the reader's understanding for these necessary limitations; and hope that the scope of the information which has been included will give a reasonable impression of Operation "Joint Endeavour", a remarkable and unprecedented military undertaking.

Carl Schulze

Acknowledgements:
I wish to record my gratitude to all the officers, NCOs and enlisted men of IFOR units who helped me during the preparation of this book. My special thanks go to Lt.Col. Dahshaw, Major Rungay, Major Haig and Chief van de Graf of the MNDSW press office; to Lt.Col. Pernod of the MNDSE, to Major Kolken of 42nd Bn. Limburgse Jagers and Capt.Bagley of the 1st US Brigade; to a Norwegian and a Canadian press officer whose names I do not know; to Capt.Laurent of the 3e REC, Capt. Fanteux of the MNDSE press office, and the Chef d'Escadron of the EED Gironde; to the press office of the Italian Brigade, who organized an excellent military tour through Sarajevo; to the press officer of the 6th Czech Mechanized Bn.; to the CO of G Coy., 2 RCR, and Capt.Bradley of the Royal Canadian Dragoons. I do not want to leave out a British REME team who repaired the carburettor of my Mercedes, or the owners of a Mercedes garage in Tuzla who welded the sump, enabling me to continue my work; not to mention the countless others, whose help was none the less appreciated for being anonymous. Special thanks also to Britta Nurmann, whose help made this book possible.

CONTENTS

A Brief History of the War in the Balkans

When President Tito died on 4 May 1980, the main force holding several historically hostile nationalities together in the Federal People's Republic of Yugoslavia died with him. His political successors soon failed the test, increasingly favouring the interests of single national groups above the common good, and exploiting deep-seated mutual suspicions for short-term political advantage. Thus the federated republics of Yugoslavia drifted apart; and when Slovenia and Croatia - fearing the dominance of the largely Serbian regime then holding national power - declared their independence in June 1991, this process became irreversible. But the rest of Yugoslavia (in essence, Serbia and Montenegro, and the mixed province of Bosnia-Herzegovina) was unwilling to accept the loss of 51 per cent of its gross national product; and the Serbian-dominated Yugoslav People's Army was unleashed against the secessionist republics. Although the Slovenian army at that time was hardly more than a militia, it succeeded in driving back the attackers in a week, and Yugoslavia was obliged to grudgingly accept Slovenia's secession.

The situation in Croatia, however, was more complicated: unlike Slovenia, Croatia has no natural defences against the rest of Yugoslavia; and the population includes a substantial Serbian minority, which was strongly opposed to the secession. These Crotian Serbs, for their part, declared their independence of Croatia, founding the "Autonomous Serbian Republic of Krajina". With both sides raising armies, the theatre of war in Croatia took shape. There is no space and little purpose to try to summarise here the events which followed. Over a map characterised by a bewildering kaleidoscope of national pockets, a complex war began to be fought out between several competing militias and rump units of the old national army. The world looked on aghast as Europeans visited upon their former neighbours a savagery and treachery long thought banished from our continent.

Bosnia-Herzegovina declared its independence in October 1991. Despite being the historical home to populations of all the main South Slav communities (it is incorrect to refer to true ethnic differences), this traditionally tolerant province somehow managed to keep out of the war until February 1992, when fighting broke out in the Mostar area between Bosnian Serbs on one side and Bosnian Croats and Muslims on the other. The Bosnian Serbs, unwilling to live in a state dominated by other communities, declared an independent republic based on the town of Pale; Serbia proper, playing its own international game, provided

Foot patrols are important for keeping in touch with the local population - they are also dangerous, due to the thousands of unrecorded mines sown during the fighting. This British soldier - his feather hackle and shoulder title identifying 1st Bn., Royal Fusiliers - is wearing a headset, and carries in his pack the PRC 350; in Bosnia this platoon-level radio is used in a patrol role. He is armed with the standard L85A1 assault rifle. Note the green *shemagh* worn as a scarf - since the Gulf War this has remained popular with British troops in all theatres.

devious and fluctuating support; and a new chapter in the bloody story opened.

In February 1992 the United Nations had started to deploy troops into Bosnia to carry through the "Vance-Owen plan" for stabilising the situation in Croatia. A second UN contingent was deployed in June 1992 to monitor the numerous ceasefires which were periodically declared (and as often broken) in Bosnia. In April 1993 the union between the Muslims and the Croats broke down, and in spite of all the UN's efforts the war raged on fiercer than ever. The fighting between Croats and Muslims ended in March 1994 with the establishment of a grudging but pragmatic anti-Serb federation between the two.

In the early autumn of 1995 the tables began to turn. Military setbacks suffered by the Serbs (always strong in

3

Canada has historically made generous contribution to UN peace-keeping operations, and played her part in UNPROFOR; for Canadian troops to be deployed without the familiar light blue berets is less common. **This corporal of 2nd Bn., Royal Canadian Regiment mans a checkpoint, armed with the 5.56mm C7A1 assault rifle by Diemaco fitted with a x3.4 Wildcat optical combat sight.**

heavy weapons but relatively weak in infantry, and now overstretched); a more aggressive posture adopted by the UN and NATO, prompted by international opinion horrified by the reported atrocities; ruined economies, and simple war-weariness amongst the civilian populations; determined US efforts in seeking a diplomatic solution - all these led to a peace agreement, concluded at Dayton, Ohio, in November 1995. Made wary by the countless violations of previously trumpeted cease-fires, the UN Security Council this time decided to push through the conditions of the Dayton peace agreement by military means. The agreement was formally signed on 14 December 1995 in Paris; and on 20 December authority was officially transferred from UNPROFOR (the United Nations Protection Force, which had been handicapped by a very limited humanitarian mandate) to IFOR (the International Peace Implementation Force, under NATO command and with a much more broadly defined mission).

The Peace Implementation Force

When the negotiations at Dayton culminated in the peace agreement, the way was open for the first out-off-area deployment of NATO troops since the Organisation's founding on 4 April 1949. Under the peace agreement the North Atlantic Council (NAC) authorised the Supreme Allied Commander Europe (SACEUR), on 1 December 1995, to deploy enabling forces into Croatia and Bosnia-Herzegovina. This decision demonstrated NATO's preparedness to implement the military aspects of a peace agreement and to help create the conditions for a lasting peace. On the same day SACEUR tasked the Commander-in-Chief Southern Europe to assume control over assigned NATO land, air and maritime forces as Commander IFOR, and to employ them as part of the enabling force. Movement of these forces began on 2 December.

On 5 December the NATO Foreign and Defence Ministers agreed the military plan for the Implementation Force. On the same day the Acting Secretary General announced that 14 non-NATO countries which had expressed interest would contribute to IFOR. All NATO nations with command over armed forces (Belgium, Canada, Denmark, France, Germany, Greece, Italy, Luxembourg, the Netherlands, Norway, Portugal, Spain, Turkey, the United Kingdom and the United States) pledged to contribute troops to IFOR; Iceland provides medical personnel.

The peace agreement (officially, the General Framework Agreement for Peace in Bosnia and Herzegovina) being formally signed on 14 December 1995, on the 15th the United Nations Security Council - acting under Chapter VII of the UN Charter - adopted Resolution 1031, authorising the member states to establish a multinational military Peace Implementation Force under common command and composed of ground, air and maritime units of NATO and non-NATO nations, with the aim of ensuring compliance with the relevant parts of the agreement. The member states are authorised to take all necessary measures to carry out the tasks identified by the resolution. On 16 December the NAC approved the overall plan for IFOR and gave orders for NATO to start Operation "Joint Endeavour" with the deployment of the main forces into Bosnia.

IFOR operates under NATO rules of engagement, which provide for the use of military force in case it should be necessary - a very widely-drawn mandate. This represents a fundamental change from the rules governing the former UNPROFOR units, whose ability to enforce the wishes of the international community - or even the dictates of common humanity - was regularly frustrated by local forces' ruthless exploitation of the prohibition on "blue-beret" troops opening fire except in direct self-defence.

20 December 1995 saw the transfer of authority from the commander of UNPROFOR to the commander of IFOR at 1100 hours local time; on that day IFOR had command over more than 17,000 troops. Apart from the named NATO nations the following non-NATO states contribute units to "Joint Endeavour" under NATO command: Austria, Bulgaria, the Czech Republic, Egypt, Estonia, Finland, Hungary, Jordan, Latvia, Lithuania, Malaysia, Morocco, Pakistan, Poland, Romania, Russia, Saudi-Arabia, Sweden and the Ukraine.

The Mission

The mission of IFOR is to monitor and, if necessary, enforce compliance with the military aspects of the Dayton agreement. The military tasks include:
- to establish self-defence and freedom of movement
- to supervise marking of the Zone of Separation (ZOS) and the boundaries between the parties to the conflict
- to monitor and enforce the withdrawal of forces to their territories and the establishment of the ZOS
- to assume control over the airspace over Bosnia-Herzegovina and the military traffic on ground routes
- to establish joint military commissions.

The deployment of IFOR is also intended to create the secure environment necessary for the work of humanitarian agencies, and the accomplishment of the non-military aspects of the agreement, within its capabilities and the limits imposed by carrying out its military tasks.

The Implementation

On 21 December the first meeting of the joint military commission took place in Sarajevo. This commission is the central authority to which the signatories of the agreement bring their military problems, questions and appeals; it is established on different levels, so that problems which arise can be solved at the lowest possible level. Non-military problems are dealt with by the Peace Implementation Council (PIC).

The parties involved in the conflict have on the whole been co-operative, and apart from some minor incidents IFOR troops have been able to carry out their tasks without resistance. Freedom of movement has been achieved by establishing control posts on all traffic routes in Bosnia - though it has more than once been necessary to break up illegal local roadblocks. The former line of confrontation had to be marked and no unit of the parties was allowed nearer to it than two kilometres. All heavy weapons had to be withdrawn to a distance of ten kilometres from this Zone of Separation.

The parties were required to declare the location of minefields, and to clear them under IFOR supervision. Sadly, this clause of the peace agreement has proved to be virtually unworkable due to the frequent absence of any documentation as to the location or the number of mines laid. (At the time of writing the only fatal casualties suffered by IFOR troops to military causes have been soldiers killed by unmarked mines.)

All fortified positions along the ZOS were destroyed. The units of the parties involved in the conflict had to return to their barracks with all their arms and have been partially disbanded. Soldiers of foreign origin who took part in the fighting were sent back to their home countries whenever identified. Finally, large areas in Central Bosnia conquered by Croats and Muslims in their 1995 offensive were returned to the Serbs; and the Serbs handed over control of a number of smaller areas along the ZOS and some larger areas in Sarajevo to the Bosnian Federation.

IFOR Organisation

The Joint Operation Center (JOC) of IFOR is located in Sarajevo and forms the main headquarters for all IFOR

Though traditionally wary of multinational commitments, France was the leading contributor of troops to UNPROFOR. Most of her crack Marine, Airborne and Foreign Legion rapid reaction units have rotated through Bosnia since 1992, and continue to do so under IFOR. This soldier of the 1st Spahis wears the French army's new Spectra helmet, body armour and camouflage outfit, and the patch of the 6th Light Armoured Division.

operations. It is subordinate to the NATO command Allied Forces Southern Europe (AFSOUTH), which like Allied Forces Central Europe (AFCENT) and Allied Forces North-West Europe (AFNORTHWEST) reports directly to the Supreme Allied Commander Europe (SACEUR) at SHAPE. AFSOUTH is the superior command and at the time of writing Admiral Leighton Smith, USN, is also Commander IFOR (COMIFOR). Apart from two maritime components (COMNAVSOUTH and COMSTRIKE-SOUTH) and the air component (COMAIRSOUTH), IFOR is mainly made up from the Allied Rapid Reaction Corps (ARRC), which for this operation was put under command of AFSOUTH and provides the ground units.

From among the divisions it commands the ARRC chose three formations, designated as follows: Multinational Division South-West (MNDSW - based on 3rd UK

continued on page 8

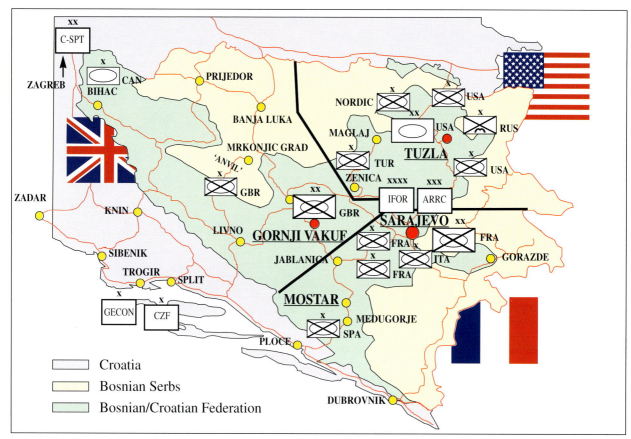

Croatia
Bosnian Serbs
Bosnian/Croatian Federation

IFOR CHAIN OF COMMAND

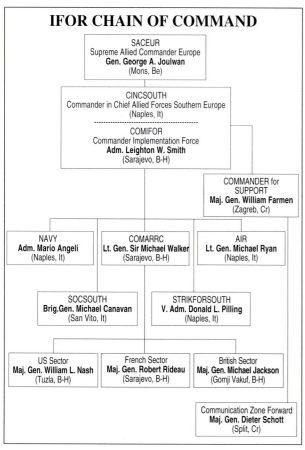

SACEUR
Supreme Allied Commander Europe
Gen. George A. Joulwan
(Mons, Be)

CINCSOUTH
Commander in Chief Allied Forces Southern Europe
(Naples, It)

COMIFOR
Commander Implementation Force
Adm. Leighton W. Smith
(Sarajevo, B-H)

COMMANDER for SUPPORT
Maj. Gen. William Farmen
(Zagreb, Cr)

NAVY
Adm. Mario Angeli
(Naples, It)

COMARRC
Lt. Gen. Sir Michael Walker
(Sarajevo, B-H)

AIR
Lt. Gen. Michael Ryan
(Naples, It)

SOCSOUTH
Brig.Gen. Michael Canavan
(San Vito, It)

STRIKFORSOUTH
V. Adm. Donald L. Pilling
(Naples, It)

US Sector
Maj. Gen. William L. Nash
(Tuzla, B-H)

French Sector
Maj. Gen. Robert Rideau
(Sarajevo, B-H)

British Sector
Maj. Gen. Michael Jackson
(Gornji Vakuf, B-H)

Communication Zone Forward
Maj. Gen. Dieter Schott
(Split, Cr)

IFOR STATES OF READINESS

state	measures taken	remarks
GREEN	- The personal equipment (weapon, helmet, flak jacket and complete belt order) can be reached within 30 minutes. - weapons are taken along when leaving base - random person and vehicle controls	- regular state of readiness
YELLOW	- all measures of state GREEN - personal equipment has to be taken along when the destination of a march is further away - command personnel always reachable - increased number of person and vehicle controls - personal equipment has to be worn	- increased threat of possible terrorist activities against IFOR personnel or facilities
ORANGE	- all measures of state YELLOW - weapons have to be carried all the time - personal equipment is carried when leaving fortified buildings - guards reinforced on command - defence positions are built - control of all vehicles and persons - guards on alarm posts on command - limited leave	- A security event has taken place. High probability of attack or terrorist activities against IFOR personnel or facilities.
RED	- all measures of state YELLOW - special security measures for persons and facilities - personnel moves to shelters on command	- attack or terrorist activities have taken place or taking place against IFOR contingents

(Right & below) One of the most striking aspects of IFOR has been the participation, under NATO command, of troops from the former Warsaw Pact. *(Right)* The 30mm 2A42 cannon of a BMD-2 air-portable armoured infantry carrier of the Russian airborne brigade serving under US command in MND North. *(Below)* More intriguing still is the brigade from the independent Ukraine, which serves under French command in MND South-East. This sniper, armed with a Dragunov 7.62x54Rmm rifle with 4x24 PSO-1 scope, scans buildings in Sarajevo for any sign of hostile activity.

Armoured Division); Multinational Division North (MNDN - based on 1st US Amored Division); and Multinational Division South-East (MNDSW - based on 6th French Division "Salamandre").

The support command, based in Zagreb, is responsible for the whole logistic support of IFOR forces. A German support contingent is stationed at Split in Croatia; this includes a transport battalion, an engineer battalion, a logistic battalion, a heliborne transport regiment, and a multinational Franco-German hospital.

The HQ of the ARRC is stationed in Sarajevo and comprises officers of all participating nations. They are supported by British units from 1 Signals Brigade, comprising 7, 14 and 16 Signals Regiments; the HQ is protected by a Turkish military police element equipped with FMC armoured personnel carriers. Also under command of ARRC are a Hungarian engineer battalion, two British engineer squadrons, a multinational special forces regiment, a British electronic warfare company, and a transport battalion consisting of Belgian, Austrian, Greek and Luxembourg troops. Special mechanical workshops from the UK and Belgium, multinational military police elements, a multinational movement control center, and all types of administrative elements complete the corps troops.

(Below) The turning-point in Bosnia came, of course, with the involvement of the US government in negotiations, and America's declared willingness to commit troops on the ground. Here Abrams tank crewmen of the 4-67th Armor fortify their checkpoint; such control posts are usually operated by a platoon of four tanks or four APCs.

(Right) Gunner of the Italian 11th "Garibaldi" Artillery photographed by an M109L self-propelled 155mm howitzer; note "Fritz"-type ballistic helmet with Fastex clip, and battery sleeve patch.

Multinational Division South-West

The MNDSW monitors the greater part of Bosnia-Herzegovina including the Bihac, Banja Luka and Jajce areas. Subordinate to the division are 2 Canadian Multinational Brigade and 4 UK Armoured Brigade. The division headquarters were located in Gornij Vakuf until 29 April 1996, thereafter at Banja Luka.

The artillery component of the division is 26 Regiment Royal Artillery, with four field batteries which were combined into two for the deployment to Yugoslavia: 150 (Colenso) Battery reinforces 17 (Corunna) Bty., and 16 Bty. (Sandham's Company) reinforces 127 (Dragon) Bty.; additionally, 52 (Niagara) Bty. of 4 Regt.RA was assigned to the regiment. Each of these field batteries is armed with six AS90 self-propelled 155mm howitzers, and divides into two field troops with three howitzers each. A fourth field battery was assigned to the regiment: 19/5 Bty., which normally belongs to AMF(L), and has eight 105mm Light Guns. 55 (The Residency) Bty. is also under command of 26 Regt., providing the HQ element and target acquisition radar. The regiment numbers 750 altogether.

38 Engineer Regiment provides support at divisional level, comprising 5 and 11 Field Squadrons and 15 Field Park Squadron, Royal Engineers. 5 Field Sqn. was assigned from 22 Engineer Regt. to replace 51 Field Sqn. (Airmobile), which deployed to Bosnia in 1995 as a part of 24 Airmobile Brigade. After IFOR took over from UNPROFOR a large number of new quarters were needed, which provided a special challenge for the regiment. It is also in charge of the maintenance of essential roads and has constructed many temporary bridges.

9 Regiment, Army Air Corps, with Lynx anti-tank and Gazelle reconnaissance helicopters, provides divisional air support, reinforced by six Chinooks of the RAF's Helicopter Support Force and four Sea Kings of 845 NAS, Royal Navy.

4 and 14 Regiments, Royal Logistic Corps are assigned to the division. The HQ personnel of MNDSW number 250, mainly from the HQ of 3 (UK) Armoured Division and the signals regiment assigned to MNDSW. Soldiers of the Royal Gurkha Rifles are responsible for the protection of the divisional HQ and other garrisons of divisional troops. Additionally the division commands units of the Royal Military Police, REME Workshops, Tactical Air Control Parties, medical facilities up to the size of a field hospital, and Explosive Ordnance Disposal teams.

4 (UK) Armoured Brigade

The brigade's operational area is the eastern part of the divisional area. It commands two British battle groups, based in early 1996 on 1st Battalion Royal Regiment of Fusiliers, and 2nd Battalion The Light Infantry. 1RRF is equipped with Saxon wheeled armoured personnel carriers, of which each of the three rifle companies has eleven. The battalion's support company has eight 81mm mortars, eight Sabre tracked armoured reconnaissance vehicles, and 20 Milan anti-tank guided weapon systems. The battalion is stationed at Sipovo; in March 1996 it was due to hand over to 1st Bn. The Queen's Lancashire Regiment.

One troop of The Queen's Royal Hussars with four Challenger MBTs has been assigned to 2LI, the battalion

(Right) Armoured Composite Land Rover of a British liasion team, fitted with a specially protected compartment, bulletproof windows and wire mesh; there is a roof hatch for an observer when patrolling. The vehicle is based on the Land Rover Defender chassis, and modifications include an explosion protection system for the fuel tank.

A soldier of the 1st Royal Fusiliers guides a Saxon wheeled APC into the transport park of the battalion's base at Sipovo. The 11.7-ton Saxon has a two-man crew and can transport eight infantrymen. With a top speed of 96km/h (60mph) and a road range of 480km (300 miles), it is a useful patrol vehicle on reasonable surfaces, though less suited to mountain tracks. For Bosnia the vehicle is fitted with the 7.62mm GPMG turret sometimes seen on the old FV432 APC, and cable-cutters to protect the commander from dangling wires.

handing over one of its three rifle companies in return, each of which is equipped with 14 Warrior armoured infantry fighting vehicles. The battalion is stationed to the east of Banja Luka, with one company at Krupa. A Milan platoon of three Warriors each with two Milan systems has been assigned to each of the companies. An artillery reconnaissance team uses another Warrior. A mortar platoon with nine FV432 tracked armoured carriers with 81mm mortars, and a recce platoon with eight Scimitar CVR(T)s, complete the battalion's assets. In March 1996 2LI handed over its mission to the 1st Bn. Worcestershire & Sherwood Foresters Regiment.

Additionally the brigade has under command an armoured reconnaissance squadron. B Squadron The Light Dragoons has three sabre troops each with three Scimitars and a Spartan APC for the troop commander; each troop includes an interpreter for contact with local liaison officers. The squadron HQ has two Sultan command post vehicles, a Samaritan armoured ambulance and a Spartan. Two additional Spartans and a Samson ARV form a maintenance and repair troop.

Engineer support is provided by 32 Armoured Engineer Regt. with 26 and 77 AE Sqns., an HQ squadron and workshops. 26 Sqn. numbers 180 and has eight Spartan carriers, seven armoured vehicles Royal Engineers (AVREs) and seven armoured vehicle-launched bridges (AVLBs). 77 Sqn., with 160 personnel, was transformed into a field squadron for deployment to Bosnia and has FV432 carriers. Combat Engineer Tractors are in use by both squadrons.

Two non-British units are subordinate to the brigade: 42nd Dutch Mechanized Infantry Battalion (the "Limburg Jagers"), and a Malaysian infantry battalion (see below).

The brigade HQ of 4 Armd.Bde. numbers 129, including the members of 204 Signals Sqn.; this squadron provides two armoured communications troops.

Queen's Royal Hussars Battle Group

The Queen's Royal Hussars are subordinate not to 4 (UK) Armd. Bde. but to 2 Canadian MN Brigade. The HQ, Alpha and Bravo Squadrons, the Recce Troop and a logistic element are deployed to Bosnia. Each of the two sabre squadrons has 12 Challenger Mk.1 MBTs; the HQ has another two main battle tanks; and the Recce Troop has eight Scimitars. The battle group handed over one troop of B Sqn. to 2LI in exchange for one rifle company with 14 Warriors. G Company, 2nd Royal Canadian Regiment is also subordinate to the battle group.

42nd Dutch Mechanized Battalion (Limburgse Jagers)

The Netherlands troops operate in the north-east part of the MNDSW and are commanded by 4(UK) Armd.Bde. (whose black-on-drab "desert rat" shoulder patch they sometimes wear). The 42nd Mech.Bn. provides the main part of the Dutch IFOR contingent. The battalion consists of two armoured infantry companies, one tank squadron, one engineer company, a battalion HQ and an HQ and supply company. The two armoured infantry companies come from the 42nd Bn. *Limburgse Jagers,* the tank squadron from the 11th Tank Bn. at Oischot, Netherlands. In the operational area in Bosnia the organization was changed to create three equally structured mixed companies each with four Leopard 2A4 MBTs, six YPR 765 APCs and three YPR PRAT (TOW turret). Only the HQs of the companies vary; in the former tank squadron there are two additional Leopards, while two YPR 765 command post vehicles are used in the other companies.

The battalion took over former British UNPROFOR bases in the region of Vitez and Travnik; headquarters are at Sisava in central Bosnia, the three rifle companies at Jajce, Skender Vakuf and Novi Travnik. The 145-strong engineer company has two Dachs armoured combat engineer vehicles, one Biber bridge-layer, and further engineer assets. The HQ and support company has an EOD section as well as a reconnaissance platoon, a mortar platoon and a medical platoon. The mortar platoon has four 120mm tubes mounted on YPR 765s. The three sections of the reconnaissance platoon each have two YPR PRIs.

Malaysian Battalion
The second non-British unit under command of 4 (UK) Armd.Bde. is a Malaysian infantry battalion drawn from elements of the 2nd Royal Ranger Regt., 4th Royal Armoured Regt. and 11th Special Service Regt., stationed at Glamoc.

The battalion has two infantry companies each with 19 M113 APCs, in three six-vehicle platoons and an HQ. Apart from the .50cal. machine guns on the M113s automatic grenade launchers are issued at platoon level; the infantrymen are armed with Steyr AUG assault rifles and Heckler & Koch light machine guns and M72 LAW66. Two armoured reconnaissance companies have 28 Condor wheeled APCs; each company's three platoons have four Condors each, three of them armed with an MG turret (2 x 7.62mm GPMG) and one with a 20mm turret; company HQ has the two remaining Condors together with wheeled vehicles.

For combat support there is an anti-tank platoon with four portable anti-tank weapon systems and a mortar platoon with six 81mm tubes. The battalion, which was already in action in Bosnia under UNPROFOR, also has signals, engineer and repair companies, a medical platoon and a national support element.

Canadian IFOR Troops
The British MNDSW has under command 2 Canadian Multinational Brigade, which is led by a Canadian brigade HQ and includes, apart from Canadian troops, Czech and British elements. Before the Canadian troops joined IFOR part of them were already deployed to Bosnia under UNPROFOR. Brigade HQ are located at Coralici; the 264 personnel are from the HQ of 2 Mech.Bde. at Petawawa, Ontario, as well as from its signals company.

The complete Canadian IFOR contingent comprises 1,000 soldiers divided into an armoured reconnaissance company,

A Fusilier (note battalion patch on the DPM cover of his Mk.6 ballistic helmet) watching civilian traffic during a stop in a town in the "Anvil" area west of Sipovo shortly before it was to be handed back from Croats to Serbs.

a mechanized infantry company, an engineer company, a military police platoon, a medical platoon and a national support element; 960 men belong to the brigade, the remaining 40 officers serving with the IFOR command structure. Apart from the mechanized infantry company all units, including the brigade HQ, come from Petewawa.

The reconnaissance element of 127 soldiers from A Sqn., Royal Canadian Dragoons is equipped with 22 Cougar wheeled armoured vehicles armed with 76mm cannons in three platoons and the squadron HQ, which also has four Bison wheeled APCs (2 x CP, 1 x LO, 1 x RRB). The squadron has 12 light and three medium trucks, and five additional Bisons, two of which are medical vehicles. Finally the repair company has six Bison MRTs (Buffalos).

The second Canadian fighting unit under command of the brigade is G Company, 2nd Bn., Royal Canadian Regiment, numbering 175 and originating from Gagetown, New Brunswick. The company has three infantry platoons, one support platoon, a transport section and a logistics section. The rifle platoons each have four Grizzly AVGPs, three carrying the infantry sections and one the platoon commander, an 84mm recoilless Carl-Gustav and a 60mm mortar. The infantry sections are armed with C7 rifles, Minimi LMGs, an 84mm Carl-Gustav and several M72s for anti-tank use; with the .50cal. and 7.62mm turret armament of the Grizzly, the section thus has considerable firepower. The support platoon unites an engineer section with an M113 SEVDozer, an anti-tank section with four

M113 "TOW under armour", and a mortar section with four 81mm tubes mounted in Bisons. Both the Royal Canadian Dragoons and Royal Canadian Regiment elements are stationed at Kljuc in the grounds of an old factory.

6th Czech Mechanized Battalion

The Canadian brigade is also in command of the 6th Czech Mech.Bn.(IFOR), headquartered at Donja Ljubija. The battalion consists of three mechanized infantry companies, an engineer company with five engineer platoons, a repair company, an HQ company, a medical company, and a transport and supply company. The three rifle companies are stationed at Stari Majdan, Arapusa and Brezicani - villages located on both sides of the ZOS, so that the Czechs operate in both Muslim and Serbian terrritory.

The 1st and 2nd Companies are each equipped with nine BVP-2 APCs, and a BVP-1 for an artillery observer team. The 3rd Company is equipped with ten OT-64 wheeled APCs. The Czech battalion, 834 strong, is drawn mostly from the 4th Brigade of the Rapid Reaction Forces, an elite formation which comprises two mechanized infantry battalions, one airmobile infantry battalion and one armoured artillery battalion. The Czech battalion is represented by liaison officers at both brigade and divisional level.

(Above) **The workhorse of the British infantry battalions since their first deployment to UNPROFOR: the Warrior IFV, with a three-man crew and space for a seven-man infantry section. Combat weight is 25.7 tons; the Perkins V8 TCA eight-cylinder diesel gives 550bhp and a speed of 75km/h (47mph). This is a vehicle of C Coy., 2nd Light Infantry outside the company location at Krupa; in Bosnia 2LI use the Warrior mainly for patrolling and guarding bases, but in case of need its 30mm Rarden cannon and 7.62mm chain gun provide the section with heavy firepower. Note the extra winter track fittings and the appliqué armour on front and sides.**

(Opposite below) The recce platoon of 1RRF have the Sabre, the latest version of the CVR(T) range; it differs from the Scimitar in being fitted with the Fox turret mounting an L49 Hughes 7.62mm chain gun in addition to the 30mm Rarden cannon.

(Below & below right) Capt.McGregor, commanding the 2LI recce platoon, in his place of business. Note the pylon for the GPS navigation system antenna, particularly useful for exact orientation in Bosnian conditions; the GPS box on the roof-mounted sight and the map secured with bungees; and white plastic sheets taped to the periscope for notes - grid references, call signs, etc.

(Right) One of the eight Scimitars of the recce platoon of 2LI - note regimental badge on the turret. This 7.8-ton, three-man CVR(T), with its legendarily low track pressure, is well able to cope with the worst the Bosnian terrain can throw at it. The platoon is mainly employed in monitoring the Zone of Separation and searching out suitable locations for new patrol bases, which are normally sited in abandoned factories, cafes, or other good-sized buildings.

(*Opposite top*) **Warrior MCRV of 2LI; this mechanized combat repair vehicle (FV512) has a hydraulically operated 6.5-ton crane and a 20-ton winch, which can be increased to 38 tons. The manually operated turret mounts a 7.62mm L94A1 chain gun.**

(*Far left*) **Battery command post vehicle of 26 Regt. Royal Artillery. The FV432 has long been replaced as an infantry carrier, but still serves reliably with a number of other arms of service; in the artillery role it carries BATES (BAttlefield Target Engagement System), the computerised control system into which all important data for artillery firing is entered.**

(*Left*) **This FV432 from 40 Field Regt. RA, attached to 26 Regt. for the Bosnia deployment, mounts the Thorn-EMI Cymbeline locating radar, which can detect the origin of incoming mortar fire out to a range of 20km (12.5 miles) - a**

capability highly relevant to this theatre, given the various widely publicised instances of the shelling of civilian targets.

(*Above*) **Gazelle recce/general purpose helicopter of 9 Regt., Army Air Corps landing on the pad at MNDSW, Gornij Vakuf. Left background is a Lynx Mk7 anti-tank helicopter armed with eight TOW missiles; Lynx has full night flight capababilities.**

(*Right*) **One of the Royal Navy Sea Kings assigned to 9 Regt. AAC for the Bosnia deployment lands to pick up a foot patrol. With the Chinooks of the Helicopter Support Force, the Sea Kings provide the British IFOR contingent with its heavy lifting.**

(Above) The first live firing of the AS90 self-propelled 155mm gun in an operational theatre: two troops from 26 Regt.RA carrying out a shoot on 28 Feb.1996 on an IFOR range at Glamoc.

(Left) Challenger tank troop commander of The Queen's Royal Hussars (The Queen's Own & Royal Irish); the newly amalgamated regiment retains the unique Danish-style "tent hat" of the latter. On the Union flag is a black pig, adopted by the soldiers at their home base at Fallingbostel in Germany. (It's a long story, and we don't really believe it anyway...)

(Opposite top left) The automatic loading system of the Royal Ordnance 155mm 39-calibre-barrel gun of the AS90 enables it to fire three-round "bursts" in less than ten seconds. The breech combines the speed of action associated with the sliding block principle and the robustness of the Crossley pad obturating system; it has an integral 12-round primer magazine.

(Opposite top right) Inside an AS90, the No.1 keys data into his BATES terminal, which will give him back a detailed fire mission order including elevation, bearing, charge number, and so on, adjusted for all relevant conditions.

(Right) Three-quarter view of a Challenger Mk.1 of 3 Troop, B Sqn., QRH; note the Russian-style additional fuel tanks fitted to the rear, and the reversed chevron recognition sign reminiscent of the Gulf War but retained by several national contingents in IFOR.

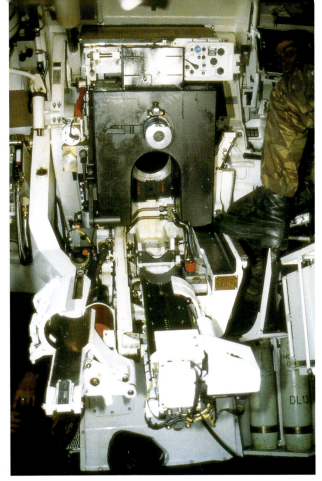

(Left) The 120mm business end of a Challenger of the QRH Battle Group, which serves under 2 Canadian MN Bde. within MND South-West; the regimental badge is just visible on the door of the thermal observation and gunnery sight (TOGS). Note that for travelling on muddy, icy roads the rubber track pads have been removed and are stowed on the turret side.

(Right) The ammunition for the Challenger's 120mm L11A5 rifled gun comes in three pieces - the projectile, the charge and the primer; 64 projectiles and 42 charges can be stowed inside the tank. The loader holds a charge; in the rack can be seen APFSDS projectiles (armour-piercing, fin-stabilised, discarding-sabot).

(Inset) Detail of the breech of the 120mm main armament.

(Below) Chieftain AVLB of 32 Armoured Engineer Regt. carrying a No.8 bridge, which can span 24.38m (roughly 80 feet). Destroyed bridges were a major obstacle to rapid deployment in Bosnia; many were temporarily replaced by an AVLB bridge while engineers rebuilt the old ones or erected Medium Girder Bridges. The regiment also operates the Chieftain AVRE with a dozer blade or mine clearance system, which is also used to fill ditches with huge fascines of maxi-fencing.

(Left) Infantryman of the Dutch 42nd Mech.Inf. Bn.(Limburg Jagers) guarding an observation post. He wears a flak jacket under the recently introduced Dutch infantry combat equipment; note the British-type DPM camouflage, and FAL 7.62mm rifle. The normal infantry section of nine men carry a GPMG, seven FALs, a Glock pistol, two Uzi sub-machine guns and three AT-4 light anti-tank weapons.

(Below) The YPR 765 APC is the workhorse of the Dutch infantry; this amphibious carrier is based on the M113, though heavily modified and fitted with laminated steel armour; it carries nine soldiers and the driver. This YPR 765 PRC OC1 is parked for maintenance. Note the additional armour on the front, which is opened here to give access to the Detroit 6V-53T diesel engine; and the toothed cable-cutter by the rear view mirror.

(*Right*) Wearing flak jacket and ballistic helmet, this Dutch infantryman scans an abandoned town during a patrol north of Travnik. Note the multinational IFOR brassard, in Arabic and Cyrillic lettering. All Dutch soldiers sent to Bosnia are professionals, not conscripts.

(*Below*) Most of the YPR 765s are armed with a .50cal.M2HB pintle-mounted machine gun in a protective "tub" turret. This vehicle guards the entrance of the Limburg Jagers' battalion HQ. Note the "Fritz"-style ballistic helmet with camouflage elastics over its cover.

(Left) This version of the YPR 765 armoured infantry vehicle is armed with a 25mm Oerlikon-Contraves KBA-B02 cannon and a co-axial 7.62mm MAG-58 MG; the turret is operated by one man and the Oerlikon gun has a dual belt-feed. The YPR 765 PRAT is also used in Bosnia, mounting a TOW turret with two launchers.

(Below left) One of the 14 Leopard 2A4 main battle tanks of the Dutch 11th Tank Bn. deployed to Bosnia. The Leopard 2 has a 120mm smoothbore gun and carries 42 rounds of APFSDS-T and HEAT-MP-T; with sophisticated day/night sighting and fire control systems, the gun is fully stabilized, and it is possible to hit a moving target while on the move - gunners are even trained to fire the main armament at low-flying helicopters. The Dutch armoured cavalry is a particularly highly-trained and motivated force.

(Right) Armed with the Austrian Steyr AUG 5.56mm assault rifle, a Malaysian infantryman guards a checkpoint. He wears the original Malaysian camouflage suit over a woollen pullover; in time the Malaysians were issued more suitable DPM arctic clothing by the British. Men from the 11th Special Service Regt. carry the XM177A1 weapon and wear a special forces combat vest.

(Below) The Malaysian troops are equipped with the Condor, a 12.4-ton amphibious 4x4 wheeled APC made by Thyssen-Henschel in Germany, carrying 12 infantry and a two-man crew. The initial version is armed with a twin 7.62mm machine gun turret. Some of the vehicles are still painted in UN white; this example is the second version of the Condor, mounting a 20mm Oerlikon cannon and co-ax 7.62mm MG in a Helio Mirror FVT 900 turret. Firing ports for individual weapons are provided in the hull sides and rear door.

(*Right*) A corporal of 2nd Bn., Royal Canadian Regiment armed with a 9mm FN35 pistol. Note the combat vest (with C7 rifle magazines in the pockets) worn over the flak jacket, and the chest patch showing nationality, rank and unit.

(*Below*) Grizzly armoured carrier outside an RCR location. This 10.5-ton section vehicle carries a crew of three and six infantrymen; it is armed with one .50cal. and one 7.62mm machine gun in a Cadillac-Gage turret.

(*Opposite top*) Company commander's Grizzly at a Canadian traffic control post; note detail of open hatches, turret and rear doors. The orange air/ground recognition panel (left) is used throughout IFOR.

(*Opposite below*) Canadian soldiers checking traffic at a control point on the former line of confrontation; for all IFOR contingents this type of duty occupies much of their time. Not all traffic is searched - freedom of movement is guaranteed under the peace agreement - and it is usually foreign vehicles which are checked. IFOR troops try to locate any remaining foreign mercenaries or other undesirables, whose repatriation is also specified by the Dayton agreement. In February 1996 a group of *mujahedin* were caught in a training camp in the French sector; in the past, such less-than-welcome volunteers for the hard-pressed Bosnian Muslim government cause proved murderously uncontrollable.

(Above) Cougar of A Sqn., Royal Canadian Dragoons. Based - like the Grizzly - on the Swiss MOWAG Piranha 6x6 chassis, this armoured recce vehicle is fitted with the same turret as the British Alvis Scorpion, armed with a 76mm L23A1 gun and a co-axial 7.62mm MG. With a crew of three, Cougars are used for reconnaissance patrols in the Bosnian countryside, where they have proved their cross-country capabilities.

(Left) Detailed view of the ceramic armour specially added to all Bison, Grizzly and Cougar vehicles. A velcro-type strip is taped onto the vehicle hull; the ceramic tiles are fastened to this, and a plastic mat is fastened over the tiles - this serves as a dust cover, and retains the camouflaged appearance.

(Right above & below) The amphibious, 13-ton, 8x8 Bison 81mm mortar fire support vehicle is based on the American LAV; in addition to the C3 mortar it is armed with a 7.62mm machine gun. It carries a crew of four, and up to 90 HE, smoke and illumination rounds for the mortar, which has a range of 5,800m (3.6 miles). This Bison, one of four serving with the mortar section of G Company's large support platoon, was photographed ready to support an infantry section during a patrol task north-east of Bihac. Note subdued national sleeve patch, and combat vehicle crewman's helmet.

(Below) Side view of a BVP-2 parked outside the Czech 1st Company base at Stari Majdan. The 2nd Co., also equipped with the BVP-2, is stationed at Arapusa, and the 3rd Co., with the OT-64 carrier, at Brezicani. The track skirt damaged in an accident reveals that the spacing between the fifth and sixth track rollers is wider than between the others. BVP-2 is the Czech name for the Russian BMP-2, armed with a 30mm 2A42 cannon and a 7.62mm PKT; it is also possible to mount an AT-5 Spandrel or AT-4 Spigot on the turret roof. The UDT-20 six-cylinder direct-injection diesel gives the 14.3-ton vehicle a top road speed of 64kp/h (40mph). After erecting a trim vane stowed on the glacis plate the vehicle is fully amphibious. Note also the three 81mm smoke grenade dischargers on each turret side; it is also possible to create a smoke screen by injecting diesel fuel into the exhaust.

(Right) Wearing the maroon beret now common to most nations' airborne forces, this member of the Czech 6th Mech.Bn. of IFOR obviously comes from the Czech Republic's 4th Rapid Reaction Brigade. On his left sleeve he displays his national title (in English) and flag patch, and the IFOR badge common to all contingents. Note the small orange box in his flak jacket pocket - this contains a specially issued first aid kit.

(Above) The Czech OT-64C(1) - (SKOT-2A) - as used by the 3rd Co., 6th Mech.Bn., is an 8x8 wheeled APC with a combat weight of 14.5 tons; a Tatra 928-18 V8 diesel engine gives a top road speed of 94kph (58mph). On the roof a one-man manually operated turret mounts a 14.5mm KPVT MG and a co-axial 7.62mm KPT MG.

(Right) Wearing a "Fritz"-type helmet, a flak jacket in British DPM colours, and displaying the right sleeve patch of his parent formation - 4th Rapid Reaction Brigade - this Czech infantryman serving in Bosnia under 2 Canadian MN Bde. is armed with a 58V calibre 7.62x39mm assault rifle.

Multinational Division South-East

The division monitors an area of some 14,300 square kilometres which includes fiercely contested sectors such as the cities of Sarajevo, Mostar and Gorazde. The headquarters of the Bosnian Serbs at Pale also fall within the operational area of the division, which is cut in two by a 400km long section of the ZOS. The division is under French command; until the end of April 1996 its HQ was in Sarajevo, but in May it moved to the airport at Mostar. As usual in French practice, the temporarily assembled task force division is named after its commander, General Robert Rideau, but it also bears the name *"Salamandre"*. Divisional HQ elements come from the 6th French Light Armoured Division, a permanent formation of the *Force d'Action Rapide*. The fighting units of the division are a Spanish brigade stationed at Medugorje; two French brigades at Mostar and Rajlovac; an Italian brigade in Sarajevo; and a Ukrainian mechanized battalion. The divisional support units are divided between Sarajevo and Mostar.

For an armoured reconnaissance component the divisional commander has the *Escadron d'Éclairage Divisionnaire ("Escadron de Gironde")*, originally stationed at Mourmelon in France; the naming of the squadron after a region of France is unusual. Apart from three RASIT battlefield acquisition radars the 150-strong EED has 39 VBL light armoured recce vehicles, the three recce platoons each having 11 vehicles: three two-vehicle sections, one Milan section with three VBLs, and the HQ section with two.

The division also commands an artillery battalion of 500 men; its two batteries each of eight GCT 155mm SP howitzers are stationed to the north of Mostar and on Mount Igman outside Sarajevo, their arcs of fire covering the whole divisional area. The division's 650-strong engineer battalion operates two mine-clearing vehicles, 20 MPG all-purpose field engineer vehicles, and a range of other engineer vehicles. An Army Light Aviation element with ten Gazelle and ten Puma helicopters, and a logistic regiment, complete the divisional troops.

French Brigade Alpha

With 1,080 personnel, this is also named *"Brigade Champeau"* after its commanding general; the HQ is located at Mostar. Subordinate to the brigade are a reinforced infantry battalion with elements of other units. The main weapon system of the battalion is the VAB wheeled APC. Before April 1996 the main fighting strength was provided by two units of the French Foreign Legion: the *2e Régiment Étranger des Parachutistes* and the *3e Escadron, 1er Régiment Étranger de Cavalerie*.

Standing guard on one of the main roads in Sarajevo, a soldier of the 1er Régiment des Spahis wears the latest French body armour with an added abdominal plate. This model of flak jacket has integral straps and D-rings for the direct attachment of personal equipment. He is armed with the standard FAMAS 5.56mm assault rifle, and wears the three-colour camouflage fatigues gradually introduced over the past three years to replace the old green "treillis F1" worn since the 1960s. The 1er Spahis, though retaining for traditional reasons the title of the former North African cavalry regiments, are today a mechanized infantry unit.

More than 1,000 legionnaires of the 2e REP (from Calvi, Corsica) are stationed in Mostar, Jablanica, Velo Polje and Koblijaca. The four infantry companies each have three platoons with four VABs; and an HQ and support platoon including an anti-tank section with two Milan systems, an anti-aircraft section with two VAB-mounted 20mm cannon, and a mortar section with two 81mm tubes. The support company has a mortar platoon with six 120mm wheeled mortars, a Milan platoon with eight Milan posts on four VABs, and a reconnaissance platoon with VBLs. The regiment has temporarily exchanged one infantry platoon for a troop of the 3e/1er REC.

The 3e/1er REC (from Orange, southern France) divides into three troops each equipped with three AMX 10RC armoured recce vehicles and three VBLs. Its HQ and services troop has four VABs - two command vehicles, one medical and one repair.

The units described above were replaced in April 1996 by

French VAB armoured personnel carrier in the command post configuration, armed with a .50cal. (12.7mm) machine gun. The amphibious, 13-ton VAB is the main APC used by the French forces in Bosnia, in a variety of configurations; the Renault turbo-charged six-cylinder diesel delivers a maximum speed of 92kp/h (57mph). The basic infantry version, VAB VTT, has a crew of two and carries ten infantrymen.

a combat unit assembled from soldiers of the *1er, 2e* and *3e Régiments d'Infanterie de Marine,* stationed in Mostar, Vrapcici, Jablanica, Sistica, Kalinovic and Klujna.

French Brigade Bravo

Stationed in Rajlovac, a suburb of Sarajevo, the brigade commands two French infantry battalions and the Ukrainian Mech.Inf.Bn.; brigade HQ is manned by personnel of the *11e Division Parachutiste* and the *35e Régiment d'Infanterie.* One of the infantry battalions, the *1er Régiment des Spahis,* is stationed on Sarajevo airport; it numbers 800 and has 90 VAB, 47 VBL and 12 Sagaie ERC 90 armoured vehicles as well as various all-terrain vehicles and trucks. The other unit, designated the 4th Infantry Battalion, is drawn from members of the *21e Régiment d'Infanterie de Marine* and *35e Régiment d'Artillerie Parachutiste;* stationed in Rajlovac, the 950-strong unit has 79 VABs, 21 VBLs and 10 Sagaie ERC 90s.

Ukrainian Mechanized Infantry Battalion

Previously an UNPROFOR unit, this 500-strong battalion comes from Dnepropetrovsk in the eastern Ukraine; it comprises two rifle companies, an HQ company, a repair and supply company and a medical company. Subordinate to the HQ company are an engineer platoon, a signals platoon, and a reconnaissance platoon with two BRDMs and two BTR-70s. Each of the two rifle companies is made up of three platoons with three BTR-70s each, and a company HQ with two more; a support section with two AGS-17 automatical grenade launchers is transported by another BTR-70. The companies are completed by a signals section and a repair section. Overall there are 33 BTR-70s, two BRDMs, 12 all-terrain vehicles, 30 heavy trucks and 40 special purpose vehicles in service with the battalion, which enables the unit to operate without outside support for a longer period (obviously, spares and replacements are not compatible with NATO stocks).

Spanish Brigade

The Spanish Brigade numbers 3,000 (actually made up of 1,750 Spanish and 1,250 Moroccan soldiers), stationed on the territory of both the Bosnian Federation and the Bosnian-Serb "Republika Srpska". The brigade is based at Medugorje and comprises one Spanish and one Moroccan mechanized infantry battalions. The Moroccan battalion has mainly French equipment, including 13 AMX 10RC wheeled armoured recce vehicles and 48 VAB APCs.

The companies of the 390-strong Spanish battalion are stationed in Mostar and on Serbian territory at Nevesinje. This *Batallon de Casadores de Alta Montana 3./64* has 52 BMR wheeled APCs, four of which mount 120mm mortars and six 81mm mortars. The battalion's three rifle companies each have three platoons with four BMR each; additionally each company has a mortar section with two 81mm tubes, and an HQ section. The support company comprises a heavy mortar platoon with four 120mm tubes, an anti-tank platoon with four Milan posts, a signals platoon, and a recce platoon with four BMR carriers. Apart from battalion HQ, the HQ and services company has one medical, one repair, one supply and one transport platoon.

Further fighting units of the brigade are a reconnaissance squadron with 16 VEC wheeled armoured vehicles, located at Dracevo; and a 270-strong mixed armoured recce contingent with 32 VECs and 15 BMRs. An artillery battery of 130 soldiers mans eight 105mm howitzers stationed at Dracevo. The logistic elements - signals, engineer, repair and medical - are headquartered at Mostar airport, often with dispersed sub-units supporting the various brigade bases.

Italian Brigade

The third formation under French command is the Italian brigade, numbering 3,500; its HQ, the so-called "Zetra Base", is located in eastern Sarajevo near the ruined Olympic ice stadium. Also under command of the brigade is a Portuguese paratroop battalion of 900 men, stationed at Rogatica.

With 760 all ranks, the strongest component of the brigade is the 8th Mechanized Bersaglieri Regiment stationed in the Vogoska and Grbavica districts of eastern Sarajevo; it is equipped with M113 (VCC1) tracked, and 6614 and VMP 90 wheeled APCs. Apart from the HQ company the 8th Bersaglieri have three rifle companies each with 13 VCC1s, three for each of the three platoons and one for company HQ; a fourth rifle company equipped

(Top) The "Sarajevo taxi" - a VBL reconnaissance vehicle, here from the divisonal recce squadron (EED "Gironde") of the MNDSE. With a crew of two or three, this 3.6-ton, fully amphibious, all-purpose light armoured vehicle is powered by a Peugeot four-cylinder turbo-charged diesel and can reach 95 kp/h (60mph) on the road; Magellan GPS satellite navigation was fitted for the Bosnia deployment. The VBL is used by the French forces with a variety of different weapons mounted; this one has a 7.62mm F1, while others have a one-man SAAM turret for a 12.7mm (.50cal.) machine gun.

(Above) Through the sight of his Milan ATGW system a soldier of a French recce unit watches the traffic on a road below his hill position. The VBL can carry six Milan rounds, and 3,000 rounds for the 7.62mm F1 machine gun.

with 35 VMP 90s; and a support company with eight 120mm mortars and 24 Milan systems.

An armoured recce company from the 19th Guides Cavalry Regt. has 12 Centauro wheeled vehicles; and a 185-strong battery of the 11th "Garibaldi" Artillery Regt. serves eight M109L SP howitzers. Controlling one of the most dangerous zones of the Bosnian theatre of war, the Italians regularly mount operations against snipers by members of the "Tuscania" Parachute Police Bn. and the 8th Parachute Regt. "Colonel Moschin" - elements of the Italian army's special forces.   Further reinforcement is provided by a company of the 131st Tank Regt. with 13 Leopard 1A5 main battle tanks. The 70-strong tank company is stationed in Sarajevo; like the logistics battalion and the artillery regiment it hails from Persano in Italy, whereas the brigade HQ and the 8th Bersaglieri are from Caserta.

An Italian engineer company is stationed at Kakanj with mine clearance and bridging equipment and diggers. The Italian field hospital is at Vogosca. There are also a logistics battalion; and 700 men serving with the national support element of the brigade, which is located in the Zetra Base.

(Top & right) **This Giat 155mm GCT self-propelled gun of one of the two French divisional artillery batteries was photographed on Mount Igman, the strategic feature dominating Sarajevo. Manned by a crew of four, the 42-ton vehicle is based on an AMX 30 tank chassis and powered by an Hispano-Suiza HS 110 12-cylinder multi-fuel engine. The maximum range is 29 km (18 miles). The gun has an automatic loading system; 42 projectiles and shell cases are carried in the rear of the turret, from which rounds of various types (HE, smoke, etc.) can be selected by the gunner and automatically loaded, with the option of single shots, or "bursts" of six rounds in 45 seconds.**

(Right) **The commander keys a fire command into the fire control computer.**

(Above) Legionnaires of a 3e/1er REC reconnaissance team - a VBL and an AMX 10RC, both with the squadron badge painted high and central - investigate small mountain tracks north-west of Jablanica.

(Right) This Legion Cavalry NCO wears the GoreTex overjacket of the new French camouflage outfit; the desert scarf, the Legion's shrunken green beret with off-set grenade badge, and the aviator sunglasses are all popular affectations among the "Royal Foreigners".

(Above) The AMX 10RC, classed as an armoured recce vehicle, is in all but name a wheeled tank. Its 105mm semi-automatic gun can fire HEAT, HE and APFSDS, and 38 rounds are carried; the turret is equipped with a SAMM CH49 electro-hydraulic control system. The vehicle has a combat weight of 16 tons, a road speed of 85kp/h (52mph) and a cross-country speed of 40kp/h (25mph), and its performance off-road is comparable to that of tracked vehicles. One 7.62mm MG is mounted co-axially with the main gun. It carries a crew of four; it is NBC-protected, and amphibious without preparation. Note here the additional armour protection for the hull; and the badge of the 1er REC on the bow plate.

(Right) Pictured during a night patrol, this Ukrainian soldier carries a 5.45x39mm AKS-74 assault rifle, fitted with a 40mm GP-25 grenade launcher - this can fire fragmentation, smoke and other ammunition out to a range of 400 metres. Note his Soviet camouflaged flak jacket and winter field uniform, now worn with the new Ukrainian nationality patch on the left sleeve.

(Above) A convoy protected by BTR-70 armoured personnel carriers of the Ukrainian Mech.Bn. moving into the suburbs of Sarajevo. The IFOR sign shares the rear plate with the former Soviet airborne forces badge from which the red star has been removed. The Ukrainian paratroopers ride on top of the vehicle in the old Warsaw Pact style.

(Right) A striking snapshot of a Ukrainian paratrooper serving with the IFOR battalion, displaying both the old and the new features of his uniform. The Soviet airborne forces light blue beret is retained, but with new Ukrainian insignia at front and side, featuring the traditional blue and yellow colours and trident symbol. The Soviet camouflage uniform is worn over the blue-and-white striped shirt retained by former Soviet airborne and other elite forces; note airborne collar badge, parachute wings on the breast, and UNPROFOR medal ribbon. Due to some unfortunate encounters between the local population and UNPROFOR in this sector, the Ukrainian paras must lay aside their blue berets for operations and wear camouflage headgear instead.

(Opposite) Armed with a CETME 5.56mm Model LC rifle, this Spanish light infantry NCO is pictured on guard in "Spanish Square" - so called for the frequency with which the Spanish contingent have to show the IFOR flag in the centre of the tragically divided Croatian/Muslim town of Mostar. Note the national flash and title and IFOR patch on his left sleeve; the white (company?) lanyard on his right shoulder; and the colourful unit insignia/rank patch worn on the chest of his flak jacket.

(Above) **BMR-600 IFV** of the Spanish contingent during a patrol in the mountains around Mostar. The 14-ton, fully amphibious BMR-600 has a top road speed of 103 kp/h (64mph). It has a crew of two and can carry 11 infantrymen, who sit along the sides facing inwards. The TC-3 cupola mounts a 12.7mm (.50cal.) M2 machine gun; the hull sides have firing ports for the infantry weapons. There are two large rear roof hatches; note locally fitted wire cages, which often hold sandbags during patrols in this bitterly polarised sector of Bosnia - the Spanish have often come under Croatian sniper fire. The whole rear hull plate opens down as a ramp, with an optional smaller door inset.

(Left) The 4.5-ton Boneschi MAV5 light armoured vehicle is used by the Italian Brigade for various purposes, including as a patrol vehicle mounting an MG3; the 3mm armoured body, with firing ports, is built on a civilian 4x4 Iveco 40.10 truck chassis. This one is providing transport for a team from the Carabinieri Parachute Bn."Tuscania", the crack MP unit of the "Folgore" Airborne Division; note Beretta 70/90 5.56mm rifle and MSG 90 sniper rifle, maroon berets, flak jacket, pistol holster strapped to the leg, and nationality/MP brassard.

These war-torn high rise blocks in Sarajevo provide ideal lairs for snipers; in one of them French special forces trapped a Serbian sniper, who died when he tried shooting his way out.

(Opposite top left) The Santa Barbara VEC (cavalry scout vehicle) of the Spanish reconnaissance units is armed with a 25mm M242 Bushmaster cannon and a co-axial 7.62mm machine gun. The 6x6 vehicle shares many components with the BMR-600 IFV and has a similar performance. The crew consists of driver, commander, gunner, and two observers who are carried in the rear hull compartment.

(Opposite top right) One of the four 120mm mortars of the

Spanish battalion's support company mounted in its BMR-600 Model 3650/59E carrier. Note the badge on the green beret of the Batallon de Casadores de Alta Montana 3./64, combining the rifle and buglehorn of the infantry with the ski and ice-pick of mountain troops. Just visible under his flak jacket is a purple lanyard. The 120mm M-86 mortar employs the M120-13 barrel. From inside the vehicle it is possible to fire out to a range of 8km (nearly 5 miles) at a rate of some 20 rounds per minute.

(Above) Leopard 1A5 IT of the Italian 131st Tank Regt. pictured on a hill in the north-eastern outskirts of Sarajevo. The Leopard 1A5 has a combat weight of 43 tons and is armed with the L7A3 105mm gun; it has a co-axial MG3 7.62mm MG, and a second on the turret roof. Note the additional armour on the turret, which is fixed to all Leopard 1A5 versions; the large sight ahead of the cupola for the passive thermal imaging system; and the TRP 2A zoom periscope in front of the commander.

(Above & opposite top) The Italian Centauro B1 - a 28-ton, 8x8, four-man armoured recce vehicle of which 12 are attached to the 8th Bersaglieri from the 19th Guides Cavalry. With a road speed in excess of 100kp/h (62mph), it mounts a fully stabilized Otobreda 105mm 52-calibre rifled gun which accepts all NATO tank ammunition which can also be used in the L7 and M68 guns; 40 rounds are carried. The computerized day-and-night fire control system, with panoramic sights for the commander, laser transceiver and thermal imaging unit, enables the crew to destroy moving targets under any light conditions. Note additional passive armour on the hull and turret; and details of the external MG3 machine gun mounts, and the gunner's roof-mounted sight.

(Left) Under command of the Italian brigade are elements of the "Colonel Moschin" Regt., a special forces unit. Carrying Minimi 5.56mm light machine guns, MP5/SD3 9mm sub-machine guns, and SG1 7.62mm sniper rifles (as illustrated), and wearing special combat vests, these highly trained troops are employed for hazardous missions - weapons searches in insecure areas of Sarajevo, patrols in mined sectors, and counter-sniper operations.

(Right) The 8.5-ton Fiat-Otobreda Type 6614 amphibious light APC/recce vehicle is armed with a .50cal.MG and can carry up to ten men. The complete vehicle is fitted with appliqué armour. For patrols in Sarajevo the soldiers usually face outwards from the rear hatch with weapons ready to engage; though the 6614 has firing ports on each side and in the back, half of these have been covered by the appliqué armour.

Multinational Division North

The core of MNDN is the US 1st Armored Division ("Old Ironsides"). Headquarters are at Tuzla, on an old Yugoslav airbase which has been massively extended by the US forces. The division commands six brigades, in which troops from a number of nations - some of them former Cold War opponents - work together. Apart from the two US mechanized brigades (1st and 2d Brigade Combat Teams), the US Aviation Brigade, and a reduced artillery brigade subordinate to the division, there are also a Russian brigade; a Turkish brigade; and a mixed brigade of Scandinavian and Polish soldiers.

The division, also named "Task Force Eagle", numbers about 20,000 soldiers, of which 8,200 are stationed in Bosnia-Herzegovina; 7,000 American soldiers based in Hungary and 5,000 in Croatia are responsible for the supply and support of the fighting units. These include not only logistic elements but also engineer troops, who constructed, e.g., the two 600m pontoon bridges across the Sava.

The divisional troops include an artillery brigade with two armoured artillery battalions; A Battery, 94th Field Artillery with MLRS; and C Bty., 333d FA with target acquisition capabilities. The two artillery battalions (2d Bn., 3d FA, and 4th Bn., 29th FA) are assigned to the two brigade combat teams, each with 24 M109A3 155mm SP howitzers. The engineer brigade has three engineer battalions, a heavy engineer battalion, and four bridge-building companies. Two of the engineer battalions, the 23d and 40th, are assigned to the brigade combat teams.

Other divisional assets include the 501st MP Co., 141st Signal Bn., three Military Intelligence battalions, elements of 5th Air Defense Artillery Bn. (two platoons with Bradley Stinger and an Avenger platoon); the Divisional Support Command (with 47th & 501st Support Bns., 123d Main Support Bn., 127th Aviation Support Bn.); parts of a Corps Support Group, a field hospital and an anti-NBC platoon.

The 4th Aviation Bde.("Iron Eagles") of the 1st Armored Division combines the 2d, 3d and 7th Bns., 227th Aviation Regt. and the 1st Sqn., 1st Cavalry, which was assigned to the 1st Brigade Combat Team in Bosnia. Apart from numerous UH-60 Black Hawk transport helicopters the brigade fields 48 Apache attack helicopters, of which 24 are assigned to 2-227 AVN and 24 to 3-227 AVN.

For the protection of divisional facilities and as a division reserve the MNDN has command over 3-325th Airborne Combat Team from Vincenza in Italy - the only US airborne battalion stationed in Europe.

US Units in Bosnia
The two equally structured brigade combat teams divide as follows:

1st Brigade Combat Team
- 4th Bn., 67th Armored Regt.
- 3d Sqn., 5th Cavalry Regt.
- 1st Sqn., 1st Cavalry Regt.
- 2d Bn., 3d FA Regt.
- 23d Engineer Bn.

2d Brigade Combat Team
- 2d Bn., 68th Armored Regt.
- 3d Sqn., 4th Cavalry Regt.
- 4th Bn., 12th Infantry Regt.
- 4th Bn., 29th FA Regt.
- 40th Engineer Bn.

The 4-67 and 2-68 Armd.Regts. each divide into four tank companies and an HQ and supply company; each tank company has three platoons with four Abrams M1A1HA ("Heavy Armor") main battle tanks and an HQ platoon with two M1A1HA; the HQ and supply company has an additional two M1A1HA.

The reconnaissance squadrons (1-1 and 3-4 Cavalry Regts.) each have three armoured troops (A, B and C Troops) with nine M1A1 and 13 Bradley M3A2 armoured recce vehicles, and two troops with helicopters: D Troop with the OH-58D and E Troop with eight AH-1F Cobras. In their HQ companies each squadron has a reconnaissance platoon with Humvees, and F Troop includes a maintenance and repair component for the helicopters. 1-1 is the regular recce element of 1st Armored Division; 3-4 was specially assigned for the deployment to Bosnia.

The 4th Bn., 4th Infantry and 3d Sqn., 5th Cavalry - regardless of the names - are both mechanized infantry battalions, with four equally structured rifle companies and an HQ company each. The four rifle companies divide into three platoons with four M2A2 Bradleys each, and an HQ component with an M2A2 and an M113. The HQ company includes a mortar platoon and a recce platoon.

Nordic/Polish Brigade
The Nordic/Polish Bde. combines 3,600 soldiers from units of eight nations, and is located north of the Turkish Bde.; 154km of the former line of confrontation lies in its

(Above left) Photographed on "Sniper Alley", in front of the Tito Barracks in Sarajevo city, a VCC1 of the 8th Bersaglieri. Fitted with additional pierced steel armour as protection against AP ordnance, this 12-ton M113-based APC has a roof-mounted .50cal.MG in an armoured "tub" position. It carries two crew and seven infantrymen, one of whom is seen here; he carries a Beretta 70/90 5.56mm rifle, wears camouflage fatigues and body armour, and sports the traditional black feather plume of the Bersaglieri on his combat helmet.

(Left) The Italian brigade's M109L 155mm self-propelled howitzers are equivalent to the M109A3, but with a 39-calibre barrel fitted with a revised muzzle brake, the maximum recoil increase being only 100mm. The 25-ton gun has a six-man crew; range with standard ammunition is 24km (15 miles), with rocket-assisted rounds 30km (18.5 miles). This gun of the 11th Artillery watches over a hill in the background where the huge cemeteries of Sarajevo have grown relentlessly - the siege is reckoned to have cost 10,000 lives.

operational area, which reaches the Sava river in the north. Apart from Denmark, Finland, Norway, Sweden and Poland, the Baltic states of Estonia, Latvia and Lithuania have each provided one symbolic platoon to the brigade since April 1996.

Apart from a Danish HQ company the brigade includes a 544-strong Danish mechanized battalion with ten Leopard 1A5 MBTs, 17 M113 APCs and two M113s with 20mm turrets. The second Scandinavian mechanized battalion is the Swedish, which numbers 752 in three mechanized companies, each with five SISU wheeled APCs and ten Pbv 302 APCs. The Polish battalion has three mechanized companies, of which two are equipped with 18 BRDM wheeled APCs and the third with ten BMP-2 APCs; the support company has six 82mm mortars, two Dana 9D 152mm SP gun-howitzers, and two Fagot ATGW systems.

For its mission the brigade is further reinforced by a Finnish engineer contingent; a logistic battalion and a medical company from Norway; and a multinational MP company. A battery with eight M109 SP howitzers has been assigned from the US divisional artillery.

Turkish Brigade

The brigade, 1,477 strong, has a 900 square kilometre operational area in the south-west corner of the American sector. It is based on a 671-strong mechanized infantry battalion equipped with 40 FMC APCs (a version of the M113 not unlike the Dutch YPR 765); the support element has six Milan 2 ATGW systems, 12 81mm and six 106mm mortars. This battalion, which previously served under

(Above & above right) "Chaos", an M1A1HA Abrams tank of C Co., 2d Bn., 68th Armor, 2d Brigade Combat Team, guards a road block in the wooded hills around Olovo, in scenes reminiscent of the Battle of the Bulge. Note the IFOR, chevron, and individual tank number 63 marked on side skirts and turret plates; and the mass of external stowage, including rolls of barbed wire for consolidating temporary positions.

UNPROFOR, is based at Zenica. It is reinforced by an extra company for protection purposes, 187 men with ten BTR 80 wheeled APCs; and by a tank company with 13 M60A3s. The brigade has an artillery battery with six M109 SP howitzers.

Russian Brigade

One of the strangest subordination concepts within IFOR is the deployment of a Russian airborne brigade under command of the US-led MNDN. However, co-operation on the ground between the former Cold War opponents is reportedly good, and both the level of training and the motivation of the Russian soldiers are very high.

The brigade, 1,500 strong, consists of elements of the 98th Division (Ivanovo) and the 76th Division (Paskvo). It is located in the most north-eastern corner of Bosnia-Herzegovina between Tuzla and the border with "rump" Yugoslavia. Brigade HQ and the signals company are stationed at Ugljevik. The brigade has two combat units, the 1st Bn. (from the Ivanovo division) and the 2nd Bn. (from the Paskvo division). These two armoured/

(Right) **US tank crewmen of 4th Bn., 67th Armored Regt., 1st Brigade Combat Team filling sandbags to fortify their platoon position at a control post on one of the main MNDN support routes - there are no** **infantry here to do the dirty work. Ballistic helmets and body armour are worn by all personnel; note the oddly reversed US flag patch on his right sleeve - this seems to be general issue.**

mechanized airborne infantry battalions are equally structured. Both have three rifle companies; each company has three platoons of 22 men - three sections of seven soldiers each with a BMD-2, plus one HQ section vehicle. The infantry sections are armed with Kalashnikov AKS-74 assault rifles, RPKS-74 light machine guns and RPG-7 rocket launchers.

Each battalion has an HQ company, and combat support is provided by an artillery battery with four 120mm 2S9 SP howitzers. Each battalion additionally has command over a platoon with eight SA-14 anti-aircraft missile systems, an engineer platoon, a signals platoon, a medical platoon and a supply platoon. The HQ elements use BTR-ZD vehicles. A brigade reconnaissance section has four BTR-80s.

A national support element combines the engineer platoon, stationed in Lopari; a transport company; a maintenance company, including a field bakery; a surgical centre; an anti-NBC element with two BTR-80s; a supply company, and a platoon of military police. Overall the supporting units have some 310 trucks of different types, 15 BTR-Ds, four command vehicles and five additional BTR-80s.

(*Left*) Abrams of A Co., 2-67 Armor, assigned to the 4th Bn. for the Bosnia deployment, guarding the US HQ at Tuzla airbase. The 58-ton M1A1HA ("Heavy Armor") main battle tank is armed with a 120mm Rheinmetall smoothbore gun, a co-axial M240 7.62mm MG, and turret-mounted .50cal. and 7.62mm guns. Internal ammunition stowage totals 40 x 120mm, 1,000 x .50cal., and 12,400 x 7.62mm. The stabilized turret is fitted with a thermal imaging system, laser range-finder, Kollmorgen Model 939 sights, and all other equipment necessary to fight a tank battle by day or night, against any kind of target, moving or stationary; the kill ratio of the Abrams in the Gulf War was awe-inspiring. The Textron Lycoming AGT 1500 gas turbine gives a top speed of 67kp/h (42mph).

(*Right*) After night sentry duty, one of the six-man crew of an SP 155mm gun of Bravo Bty., 2-3 FA has unloaded the M2 .50cal. MG and now removes the night vision sight in the grey light of early morning.

(*Below left*) Belonging to Bravo Battery, 2d Bn., 3d Field Artillery, this M109A5 is well tucked into its fire position near Dubrave. The M109A5 mounts the 155mm M284, with a range of up to 18km (11 miles). The A5 is an improvement over the M109A2, fitted with the T154 track, a new suspension system and a more powerful engine.

(*Below*) A gunner of 2-3 FA loads the M284 gun of his M109A5 SP howitzer with a 155mm HE round. After the projectile is moved into the breech by hand it is rammed before the propellant charge is inserted.

(*Left*) M2A2 Bradley infantry fighting vehicle of B Co., 3d Sqn., 5th Cavalry Regiment. The amphibious 30-ton Bradley IFV is powered by a Cummins VTA-903T turbo-charged eight-cylinder diesel engine and has a top speed of 61 kp/h (38mph). It accomodates a driver, commander and gunner plus a six-man infantry section. The vehicle is armed with a 25mm M242 cannon, a co-axial 7.62mm M240C machine gun, and two TOW launchers on the left side of the turret. Note that sections of the armoured side skirts have been unshipped for easier access to the tracks.

(*Below & opposite*) Mud-caked M2A2 at the main entrance to the 1st Brigade Combat Team HQ. Note details of the additional armour, fitted to improve battlefield survivability, which increases the weight of the vehicle (originally 22 tons) by eight tons.

(Opposite above & below, and above) The cavalry's M3A2 differs from the M2A2 only in minor details, like the absence of firing ports and vision blocks; the M3A2 crew totals only five, and more ammunition is carried for the main armament and the machine gun. In American cavalry regiments the M3A2 is employed as an armoured reconnaissance vehicle. These are M3A2s of 1st Sqn., 1st Cavalry Regt., which have names painted on their TOW launchers - e.g."Big Kahuna". Note the view of the loaded TOW launcher swung up ready to fire (above).

(Right) The M998 Humvee is used in a variety of configurations and in great number by all American troops deployed, the range of flavours including armoured examples fitted with TOW, versions for engineers and mortar crews, and command post vehicles. This Hummer photographed at an MP traffic checkpoint near Dubrave mounts a 40mm automatic grenade launcher.

(*Left*) Armed with an M16A2 5.56mm rifle with integral M203 grenade launcher, this trooper of B Co., 3-5 Cavalry serves as a mechanized infantryman, covering his section as they search buildings in the Zone of Separation. During one of these missions an American patrol discovered a Serbian weapons compound containing artillery pieces, anti-tank weapons, ammunition and mines. Note his ammunition vest for carrying the 40mm grenade rounds; and his divisional sleeve patch.

(*Below*) A non-com of 4-67 Armor, the small black metal insignia pinned to his helmet cover identifying him as a staff sergeant/E6, standing sentry at a checkpoint - thus the fairly unusual sight of a

tanker carrying an M16A2 in addition to his Beretta 9mm pistol in a shoulder rig. Note pile-lined winter cap worn under his helmet.

(*Right*) Out by the section's Bradley, which covers the building search with its turret armament, a vehicle crewman of Bravo, 3-5 Cav receives new orders; note his non-regulation way of slinging the M16A2. Standing orders for US troops in Bosnia specify that helmet and body armour are to be worn whenever they are outside their buildings.

(*Below right*) Covered by his Bradley's turret guns, and carrying the Minimi 5.56mm light machine gun, a trooper of 3-5 Cav checks the car and papers of a Croatian driver entering a Serb-populated area of northern Bosnia.

(*Right*) The venerable M113 is still employed in a variety of versions; this is an engineer section vehicle. Additional armour on the front plate and rear-mounted armoured fuel cells are now routinely fitted to all configurations.

(*Below*) Another faithful veteran from that other muddy battlefield of long ago is the 51-ton M88A1 VTR armoured recovery vehicle, based on the M48A2 Patton tank chassis with the engine of the M60A. Its winch can haul 41 tons, its crane can lift 23 tons, and engineers and tank men have been in love with it for about 30 years.

(Above & right) Two AH-64 Apache attack helicopters of the 227th Aviation Regt. rise from the airfield at Tuzla on a misty day. The two-man, eight-ton Apache has a top speed of around 309kp/h (190mph), and is armed with a 30mm cannon, up to four Hellfire ATGWs, and pods of unguided rockets to taste. This unit's AH-64s have a red "Apache head" painted on the sides. Task Force Eagle has 48 of these battle-proven helicopters in country.

(Above) American logistic skills and resources have been as beneficial in Bosnia as the deterrent effect of American firepower. Here Belgian 7.5-ton trucks cross one of the two bridges built over the Sava river near Zubanja by the US 502d Engineer Co. ("River Rats"), 130th Engineer Bde., using ribbon bridge on floatable bridging elements. Following the disaster shortly after Christmas 1995, when the US camp near the Sava was washed away by floods and much equipment was lost, the Americans managed to complete the first of the two bridges by 31 December.

(Left) The SISUs used by the Norwegian Telemark Bn. - specially raised for international peace missions - have an armoured tub for the .50cal. gunner and an MG3 mounted in the rear compartment hatch. Note that all wear CVC helmets.

(Above right) The 15-ton Finnish-built SISU XA-180 wheeled APC is used by the Swedish (illustrated) and Norwegian troops of the Nordic/Polish brigade. This fully amphibious 6x6 vehicle is powered by a Valmet six-cylinder turbo-charged diesel; it has a crew of two and carries ten infantrymen in the rear compartment. It is armed with a .50cal. M2 machine gun on the roof; 84mm Carl-Gustav and AT-4 anti-tank weapons and ammunition are carried inside; and note the firing ports and vision blocks (three on each side) for the infantry.

(Right) As a tracked carrier the Swedish armoured infantry in Bosnia use the Pbv 302, a 13.5-ton amphibious APC which accomodates a two-man crew and ten infantrymen. The small turret mounts a 20mm Hispano Suiza cannon. Note the characteristic red IFOR chevron used by the Swedes. The Swedish soldier in front of the vehicle is armed with a 5.56mm Ak5 rifle; his fatigues are in the same type of distinctive splinter-camouflage as the Swedish vehicle paint scheme.

(Right) Turkish FMC armoured personnel carriers are based on the American M113 and are basically similar to the Dutch YPR 765. The turret mounts a 25mm Giat Industries M811 cannon and a co-axial 7.62mm MG. The amphibious 14-ton vehicle, with road speeds up to 70kp/h (44mph), can supposedly cram in up to 13 personnel. This FMC was serving with the Turkish security element guarding the ARRC HQ in Sarajevo.

(Below) The second version of the FMC used in Bosnia is the Advanced APC with a one-man turret fitted with a 12.7mm and a 7.62mm machine gun, and additional armour.

(Below) The major equipment of the Russian airborne brigade in Bosnia is the BMD-2, with its 30mm 2A42 cannon and 7.62mm PKT co-axial MG; there also is a bow-mounted 7.62mm gun, and it is possible to mount the AT-5 Spandrel ATGW system on the top right side of the turret. The 8-ton BMD-2 is air-portable and fully amphibious; the crew consists of driver, commander, and five infantrymen, two of whom sit to the left and right of the driver and the other three in the troop compartment behind the turret. The minimal space still encourages Russian soldiers to ride on top.

(Right) Stopping the author's car, this Russian paratrooper wears combined body armour and combat vest, and is armed with an AKS-74 with a GP-25 40mm grenade launcher. Note the bayonet worn on the armour vest, and the national left sleeve patch.

(*Above & left*) Armed with an RPKS-74 light machine gun to which a night vision device is fitted, this soldier is one of the two light machine gunners in his infantry section. The RPKS-74 has a maximum range of 460m, and a rate of fire of 600 to 650rpm. Note the airborne collar badges, and the contrasting camouflage schemes of the helmet cover and fatigues.

(*Right*) Another angle on the AKS-74 with 40mm grenade launcher - but the most interesting thing about this paratrooper is that he still wears the old Soviet VDV airborne forces patch on his right sleeve, as well as the new tricolour on the left.

(Above & left) Based on the chassis of the BMD-1, the 2S9 120mm SO-120 self-propelled howitzer is used in the artillery battery of the Russian brigade. Amphibious and air-portable, it has the same engine as the BMD-2, a speed of 60kp/h (37mph), a combat weight of 8.7 tons, a crew of four, and a rate of six to eight rounds of 120mm per minute out to 13km (8 miles); 25 rounds can be stored internally.

(Right) The commander of a 2S9 wearing body armour over the latest Russian camouflage uniform, with the new national sleeve patch.